"No Man Can Hinder Me"

BLACK TROOPS IN THE UNION ARMIES
DURING THE AMERICAN CIVIL WAR

An Exhibition at the Beinecke Rare Book & Manuscript Library
December 2003–February 2004

Frederick Douglass. Letter to friend.
21 November 1863. Subsequent pages
reprinted throughout brochure.

Carte de visite. Unidentified veteran.
His chevrons are those of sergeant. He is
wearing the regulation frock coat, a
shoulder sling with circular eagle plate,
and the Model 1840 non-commissioned
officer's sword. He supports a volume of
J.T. Headley's *The Great Rebellion*.

1864

+ + + + + + + + + + + + + + + + + + + +

On 12 and 13 June 1864, the Army of the Potomac abandoned its trenches near Cold Harbor and crossed the James River: its destination, Petersburg, Virginia. Located on the south bank of the Appomatox River, 10 miles above its mouth, Petersburg was linked by rail and water to the James River, the Chesapeake Bay and the Atlantic Ocean. Goods from around the world flowed through Petersburg to other parts of the Confederacy. Five railroads converged on the city and then funneled in a single line to Richmond, the Confederate capital, 23 miles to the north. If Petersburg fell, Richmond was doomed.

Grant's commanders botched several well-conceived but feebly executed attempts to take the city between 15 and 18 June. But in some of the last convulsive lunges on the 18th, before both sides dug in for a siege that neither wanted, units from the Ninth Corps, commanded by Major General Ambrose Burnside, charged across Poor Creek and seized a patch of rising ground adjacent to a Confederate strongpoint known variously as Elliott's—and less frequently, Pegram's—Salient. There the federals dug in and established a line of earthworks less than 130 yards from the rebel redoubt—closer than at any point along the Union and Confederate trenches. The position was held by the 48th Pennsylvania, whose recruits had been drawn from among the miners of Schuylkill County. Their commander, Lieutenant Colonel Henry Pleasants, was a mining and civil engineer in civilian life. The idea of digging a tunnel beneath the Confederate strongpoint and

Samuel Martin, *2nd Sergeant.*

blowing it up seems to have occurred naturally to Pleasants and his men. When they presented their proposal it was strongly endorsed by key commanders at both the division and corps levels.[1]

A breach in the Confederate defenses at this point promised tantalizing possibilities. Five hundred yards beyond the salient lay the Jerusalem Plank Road. Half a mile to the north stood Cemetery Hill in Blandford. Nothing better symbolized the strategic importance of Cemetery Hill to the Union cause than the McRae Monument, a memorial to the veterans and dead from the War of 1812, situated at the hill's crest. It is from the McRae Monument, featuring the cockade hats and armaments used by Captain McRae and his men, that Petersburg takes its moniker, "Cockade City." From Cemetery Hill, Union canon would dominate the city and the rear of the Confederate front lines.

The 48th Pennsylvania commenced digging on 25 June. As the engineering challenges were being met, Burnside devised his plan of attack. Of the four divisions under his command, the men of the Fourth Division, the only black troops in the corps, were the freshest. Burnside chose these men to lead the Union assault.[2] His plan was simple: at the moment the mine exploded, the Fourth's first brigade would dash forward and, on reaching the main Confederate line, deploy into two sections. The first would wheel to the right behind the enemy works and roll up the enemy's right flank, while the other would swing to the left on a similar mission. The second brigade would then sweep through the breach to the Jerusalem Plank Road, and after a quick march seize Cemetery Hill. Testifying later before Congressional Committee, Burnside enumerated his reasons for selecting the Fourth to lead the advance, "[The] division had not suffered so severely [as the three white divisions under his command], in fact had not been in any general engagement during the campaign, but had frequently been very honorably engaged on the outposts of the army." Burnside was further persuaded by the confidence Ferrero and his officers placed in the ability of their troops to lead the charge.

In the weeks leading up to the attack the men of the Fourth Division did more than their share of pick-and-shovel work. Despite this, they soldiered on, fully aware of the significance of their presence. "We have seen the fruits of slavery," wrote D. R. Brown of the 31st United States Colored Troops [USCT] on 18 July, "the desolation and despair of hundreds...." "We know and the slave knows," added Alexander Banks, "that fighting for the Union is fighting against slavery." Endorsing this view, other men serving in the USCT units might have expanded its perspective with pointed reference to their own experience.

+   +   +   +   +

The Union army numbered 16,367 officers and men in early April 1861. After the surrender of Fort Sumter, 13 April 1861, thousands of free black men and women rushed to answer President Lincoln's call for volunteers.

During a monster rally held at the Twelfth Baptist Church in Boston, freemen and women of Massachusetts resolved "to stand by and defend the Government with 'our lives, our fortunes, and our sacred honor.'" In Washington, Jacob Dodson—who, before his duties as a custodian in the Senate, had been three times across the Rocky Mountains on expeditions with John C. Frémont—wrote to the War Department offering the services of "300 reliable colored free citizens" for the defense of that city. From Battle Creek, Michigan, Dr. G. P. Miller wrote to the Secretary of War soliciting the privilege of "raising from 5,000 to 10,000 free men to report in sixty days to take any position that may be assigned to us (sharpshooters preferred)." All across the North, in Providence, New York, Philadelphia, and Cleveland, black men—and women prepared to serve "as nurses, seamstresses, and warriors if need be"—rushed to participate in the mobilization for war.

But in every instance government agents and local officials met the wellspring of African American participation with policies that excluded blacks from military service. In Providence, police officials warned that drilling exercises by blacks would be considered "disorderly gatherings" and threatened participants with arrest. New

York's police chief ordered black men to discontinue drilling, on the grounds that he would be unable to protect them from public wrath. "We want you d—d niggers to keep out of this," freemen were told by Cincinnati police. "This is a white man's war." Jacob Dodson received a one-sentence note from the Secretary of War, "this Department has no intention to call into the service of the Government any colored soldiers."

Antipathy towards black enlistment was no less intense within the ranks. "We don't want to fight side and side with the nigger," nineteen-year-old Felix Brannigan, a corporal in the Seventy-fourth New York Volunteers wrote to his sister. "We think we are a too superior race for that." When Company G of the First Regiment Kansas Volunteers discovered that one of their number was black, they wrote a letter to their commanding general, "We have no objection to endure all the privations we may be called upon to endure," they began, "but to have one of the company, or even one of the regiment, pointed out as a 'nigger' while on dress parade or guard, is more than we like to be called upon to bear."

Black Americans had fought in every one of the nation's previous conflicts. They had distinguished themselves in the colonial wars and in the War for Independence. Yet in 1798, the Secretaries of War and Navy issued separate orders forbidding black enlistment in the Marine Corps and on naval warships. Military necessity apparently overrode those orders, for black soldiers and sailors served courageously in the naval war with France (1798–1800) and in the War of 1812.

As war broke out between the states, policy makers, faced with the prospect of arming freemen and slaves, hesitated. Since the Revolutionary era, northern states had employed a series of legal and extralegal measures to deprive black Americans of the rights white Americans associated with citizenship. Most denied African Americans the right to vote or to sit on juries. Many also prohibited blacks from testifying against whites in court. White Americans deemed the bearing of arms in the nation's defense an essential element of citizenship, yet the Militia Act of 1792 limited enrollment to white men.

The question of whether or not to arm black soldiers during the Civil War, had implications that ranged beyond the particulars of military necessity. Enlisting black men in the federal army would not only suggest a measure of equality that northerners were unwilling to concede, it would also enlarge black claims for citizenship. As the contingencies of war reshaped federal war aims, the policies relating to black enlistment became increasingly intertwined with the politics of emancipation.

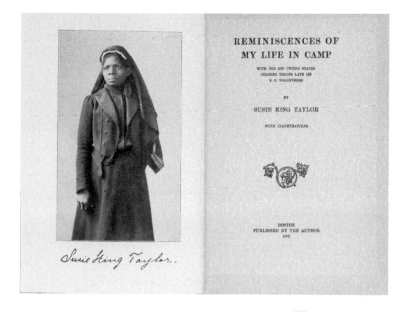

Susie King Taylor. *Reminiscences of my Life in Camp.* Boston: Published by the Author, 1902.

From the beginning, abolitionists, black and white, along with radical Midwestern free soilers insisted on black enlistment and the abolition of slavery as cornerstones of federal policy. Officially and unofficially, however, northerners were repeatedly assured that the war was in no way associated with black issues or concerns. Both houses of Congress passed legislation affirming that the war was being waged in defense of the Constitution and to preserve the Union—not to overthrow or interfere with slavery. Adhering closely to the political philosophies of his idols Thomas Jefferson and Henry Clay, President Lincoln spent the first two years of the war drumming up support for various colonization schemes to relocate African Americans to territories outside the United States. Through proposals for compensated emancipation, Lincoln also sought to pay slaveholders for their lost "property" rather than the slaves for their unrequited labor. "The existing war has no direct relation to slavery," the *National Intelligencer* summed up succinctly. "It is a war for the restoration of the Union under the existing Constitution."

Significantly, slaves themselves were among the primary movers to place the issue of their emancipation atop the national

Alfred Jackson, *Sergeant*; Wilson Weir,
Corporal; David Long, *Private*

agenda. Directly linking the war with freedom, they approached federal lines offering their lives and their labor in the Union cause.
Recognizing the enemy of their enemy as a friend (allegiances were
never quite so clear-cut; northern soldiers often turned on escaping
slaves in violence), slaves were pleased to provide information about
Confederate troop placements, assist in the construction of fortifications, and serve as guides through unfamiliar territory. "The negroes
are our only friends," General Ormsby M. Mitchel wrote the
Secretary of War in early spring 1862, "and in two instances I owe my
own safety to [them]."

Insights the soldiers gained through their interactions with
former slaves were passed on to their officers, who relayed these up
through the chain of command. In letters home, Union soldiers
informed, not only relatives about their perceptions and experiences;
they informed northern opinion. When in late fall 1861, Secretary of
War Simeon Cameron publicly advocated arming the slaves to fight
for the Union and win their freedom, Lincoln silenced him by pack-
ing him off to a ministerial post in Russia. But the secretary's com-
ments revealed how closely questions of emancipation were linked
with the issue of black enlistment and showed how keenly both were
being considered at the highest levels of the Lincoln administration.

As the Union army confronted its enemy in the field, the
indispensable role that forced black labor played in enabling the
Confederate war effort magnified the slavery issue for federal policy
makers. Slaves and southern freemen directly supported frontline
Confederate troops by constructing fortifications, transferring sup-
plies, and performing camp duties that rebel soldiers would otherwise
have had to do for themselves. Throughout the southern states this
pool of unpaid labor raised the staples necessary for foreign credit,

manufactured weapons of war, and produced the food that sustained both the military and civilian populations. As the war dragged on, even the most obtuse federal commanders came to view escaping slaves as a double asset: subtractions from Confederate strength and additions to the Union effort.

Still smarting from the humiliating Union disaster at Bull Run, and prodded by growing emancipationist sentiment in the North, Congress passed the First Confiscation Act in August, 1861. The legislation stipulated that any master who allowed his slave to work for the Confederate cause, forfeited his claim to that slave. The slave—as property, not human being—was liable to confiscation and could be held by Union forces as "contraband of war." Defining former slaves as property rather than as human beings allowed policymakers to sidestep the issue of emancipation.

But events in the field quickly outstripped congressional legislation. Without asking too closely whether or not escaping slaves had worked for the Confederacy, some Union commanders turned the potential crisis of refugees into an asset by employing fleeing slaves in the Union effort. Hundreds of thousands of former slaves supported military operations throughout the war by working in the quartermasters, ordinance and engineering departments.

Only a small step separated arguments about the value of black labor in support of Union military forces from proposals that black men be more directly engaged against the Confederacy. As northerners gradually converted to the view that Union success depended on the destruction of slavery, many, for obviously self-serving reasons, began to demand that black men take a frontline position in the struggle for their freedom.

Unauthorized individual initiatives by senior military commanders and prominent politicians further pressed the issue. General John W. Phelps, serving in the Department of the Gulf, and General David A. Hunter, commander of Union operations along the coast of South Carolina, Georgia, and Florida, armed former slaves in the summer of 1862 and pressed the War Department for recognition of these troops in the form of pay, equipage, and officers' commissions. Both commanders received public reprimands and reversals. But almost immediately following their removals, their previously unacceptable policies won official sanction. Governor John A. Andrew of Massachusetts bombarded the War Department and the president with requests for authorization to raise a black regiment. On the Kansas frontier, Senator James H. Lane requested, and then simply assumed that authority.

Northern military setbacks throughout the summer and fall of 1862 further reordered Union priorities. On 17 July 1862, Congress passed the Second Confiscation Act, a bill authorizing the president "to employ as many persons of African descent as he may deem necessary and proper for the suppression of this rebellion." The Militia Act, passed the same day, emancipated former slaves, as well as the families of those slaves, employed in the Union war effort—provided their former masters had been members of the Confederacy. The language in both acts was narrow and shifted decision-making responsibility to the president, but the legislation provided the legal foundation for the response that the president would deliver at the beginning of the following year.

As the nation approached the third year of a war that everyone had thought would have been over in just a few weeks, Union manpower shortages were becoming acute. It was now clear that prolonged warfare could not be waged with a volunteer army. Terms of enlistment for many of the men who had eagerly answered Lincoln's early calls for volunteers were set to expire. As the costly campaigns through which the Union forces gradually gained the upper hand thinned its ranks, the numbers of volunteers had plummeted. Increasingly, the military advantages of arming freemen coupled with the need to find employment for growing numbers of former slaves made the prospect of black enlistment seem like common sense.

Throughout the war, President Lincoln had sought to appease the demands of the border states (those slave states that had not seceded: Maryland, Delaware, Missouri, Kentucky), whose support he felt was crucial to successful prosecution of the war effort. His offers of compensated emancipation had been aimed chiefly at residents of those states.

On 31 December 1862, the same day that he completed revision of the Emancipation Proclamation and wrote out its final draft, Abraham Lincoln signed a contract with Bernard Kock using federal funds to colonize five thousand African Americans to Vache Island, a small island off the coast of Haiti. Without second guessing Lincoln's political calculations or racial motivations, it is noteworthy that his actions form an almost perfectly historical parallel to those taken by Congress six months earlier. On 16 July, the day before passing the Second Confiscation Act, Congress appropriated half a million dollars to support the colonization of African Americans outside the nation's borders. The juxtaposition of these two efforts—emancipation and colonization—by both the legislative and executive branches of the

Head-Quarters U. S. Forces,
Fort Myers, Fa. Oct. 8th 1864.
E. R. Moore,
          Lt. and Adjt. 2d U. S. Cold. Inf.
                    I
have the honor hereby to recommend that
Corp. Lewis McCoy Co. G 2d U. S Cold. Inf.
be made sergeant vice Sergt. Wm. R.
Murray deceased: that Pvt. Geo. Johnson
Co. G 2d U. S. Cold. Inf. be made corp.
vice Corp. Lewis McCoy promoted:
that Pvts. James H. Chapman and
Robt. Carter of Co. G 2d U. S. Cold. Inf.
be made corporals to fill original
vacancies in their company.
     Also that the above promotions
shall date from Oct. 1st 1864.
                    Your obdt. servant,
                    Consider H. Willett
                    Capt. Co. G 2d U. S. Cold. Inf.
                    Comdg. Post.

Consider H. Willett. Letter to E. R.
Moore. 18 October 1864. *Loomis-Wilder
Family Papers, Manuscripts and Archives,
Yale University Libraries.*

David Hodgens, *Corporal*; Henry Lively, *Corporal*; Kendrick Allen, *Corporal*

federal government shows just how threatened Americans were generally by the pending end of slavery.

Despite its expansive rhetoric, the Emancipation Proclamation freed no more slaves than had already been authorized by the Second Confiscation Act. It left untouched slavery in the border states, and it exempted those parts of the Confederacy already under Union control. Yet Lincoln's proclamation transformed the war in ways that only a president could. It made emancipation a centerpiece of federal war policy, and it provided for the acceptance of black soldiers and sailors in the Union armies and navy.[3] The establishment of the Bureau of Colored Troops by the War Department in May 1863 to regulate the recruitment of black soldiers and the selection of their officers signaled the full commitment of the Lincoln administration to a systematic, centrally coordinated approach to black enlistment.

Once the Emancipation Proclamation had been issued, state governors moved quickly to establish separate black regiments as a way to help fill conscription quotas. But the number of potential recruits among free black men in the North was relatively small. Much larger numbers of black men resided in the border states and in those areas of the Confederacy occupied by federal forces. Under a scheme designed to fill national quotas while at the same time leaving the northern labor force intact, northern states sent agents throughout the occupied South and the border states to recruit enlistees, crediting them toward northern state draft quotas. The 1864 amendment to the Enrollment Act authorizing this initiative specified "unemployed" men, both black and white. But recruiting agents invariably targeted black men. In their greed to collect men and the accompanying bounty, recruiters resorted to a range of high-handed tactics, including open impressment as a way to fill their lists. Black men, slave and free, were rounded up from plantations, contraband camps, city streets, and even from branches of the army where they were already employed as laborers to fill depleted Union ranks. Protests by African Americans were legion and a few countermeasures taken, but these practices continued to varying degree for the duration of the war.

Black men who served in the Union armies during the Civil War understood that their presence embodied social and political commitments far beyond the immediate demands of the war. Their experiences had taught them the contradictory impulses behind whites' acceptance of their enlistment. Those who, early on, had seized the initiative and sought to enlist along with other patriotic Americans remembered that they had been forcibly barred from doing so by a web of state and federal restrictions. From the sidelines they had watched as the muster rolls, when finally opened, did so not in response to moral suasion or official commitment or even common sense but to a grim calculus of military necessity and to white fears of conscription. Escaped slaves who joined the armed forces eager to confront their former masters on different terms quickly discovered that they had exchanged one white-dominated hierarchy for another and that this one too assumed and enforced their inferior status.

The men of the Fourth Division had been recruited from New York, Connecticut, Ohio, Indiana, Illinois, Pennsylvania, Maryland, and Virginia. Drawn from northern, southern and border states, these men represented a wide range of backgrounds and experience. For them, the assignment to lead the Union assault in what became known as the Battle of the Crater was a rare opportunity to take a front line position in a war that from the beginning they had linked with the abolition of slavery. But they also defined their performance in much broader terms. Distinguished service in the battlefield, they hoped, would engender popular support for basic recognition of their civil rights. Closely associated with these rights lay their claim for citizenship. In the parlance of the day they were determined to prove themselves men. The question hanging over the Fourth Division, as it did over all black troops fighting in the Civil War was "Can/Will They Fight?" No matter how many times that question was answered—at Port Hudson (27 May 1863), Fort Wagner (18 July 1863), Olustee (20 February 1864)—the fact that no action ever laid it to rest suggests something of the conditions under which these men fought.

+   +   +   +   +

Colonel Henry Goddard Thomas, twenty-seven years old and an attorney in civilian life, commanded the second brigade of the Fourth Division. A keen observer of camp life, Thomas recorded the men's reaction on the night they learned that they would be leading the attack in the upcoming Union assault:

> Any striking event or piece of news was usually eagerly discussed by the white troops, and in the ranks military critics were as plenty and perhaps more voluble than among the officers. Not so with the blacks; important news such as that before us, after the bare announcement, was usually followed by long silence. They sat about in groups, "studying," as they called it. They waited, like the Quakers, for the spirit to move; when the spirit moved, one of their singers would uplift a mighty voice, like a bard of old, in a wild sort of chant. If he did not strike a sympathetic chord in his hearers, if they did not find in his utterance the exponent of their idea, he would sing it again and again, altering sometimes the words, more often the music. If his changes met general acceptance, one voice after another would chime in; a rough harmony of three parts would add itself; other groups would join his, and the song would become the song of the command.
>
> The night we learned that we were to lead the charge the news filled them too full for ordinary utterance.... They formed circles in their company streets and were sitting on the ground intently and solemnly "studying." At last a heavy voice began to sing,
>
> "We-e looks li-ike me-en a-a-marchin' on,
> We looks li-ike men-er-war."
>
> Over and over again he sang it, making slight changes in the melody. The rest listened to him intently; no sign of approval or disapproval escaped their lips or appeared on their faces. All at once, when his refrain had struck the right response in their hearts, his group took it up, and shortly half a thousand voices were upraised extemporizing a half dissonant middle part and bass. It was a picturesque scene....

By 28 July, the mine was ready. The time set for the exploding gunpowder was 3:30 a.m., 30 July, a Saturday. So many rebel units had been called off to check a Union diversion threatening Richmond that on the evening of 29 July only three Confederate divisions remained in defense of Petersburg. The men of the Fourth Division waited until nightfall before advancing quietly into position. "Around us could be heard the shuffling tread of troops," Lieutenant Freeman S. Bowley of the 30th USCT recalled, "but it was so dark that nothing could be seen."

List ~~Invoice~~ of Clothing, Camp and Garrison Equipage Received ~~transferred~~ by
E. P. Rogers 1m 2o F
Lieut. ~~H. B. Beebe~~, Q. M., 29th Regt. ~~U. S. C. Troops~~, to Gen Gorden. W. Stewart
Conn Vols Colored
1st Lieut Vol A. R. Q. M. ~~for~~ 29th Regt. ~~U. S. C. Troops~~, at
Conn Vols Colored
in the field near Richmond on the 12th day of April 1865

NUMBER.		ARTICLES.	COST WHEN NEW.			CONDITION.
			DOLLS.	CENTS.		
2	Two	Forage Caps				New
21	Twenty one	pr Trousers foot				"
10	Ten	U.S. Coats lined				"
13	Thirteen	Shirts flannel				"
11	Eleven	Drawers C. F.				"
10	Ten	pr Booties				"
19	Nineteen	" Stockings				"
3	Three	Rubber Blankets				"
6	Six	Gt Coat Straps				"
4	Four	Knapsacks				"
2	Two	Haversacks				"
1	One	Canteen				"
3	Three	Shelter Tents				"

Edward P. Rogers
1st Lieut 29 Conn Vols
Comdg Co E

Lt. Edward P. Rogers, 29th Connecticut
Volunteers. *List of Clothing, Camp and
Garrison Equipage.* 12 April 1865.

+ + + + +

The timing of their enlistment had magnified blacks' expectations about the rewards of military service. Having entered the war when Union fortunes were low, African Americans recognized the important role they played in shifting its balance to the Union's favor. In return, they hoped their service would foster a greater commitment to racial equality. While contemporaries in the North and South shared this understanding of the significance of black participation, few believed that it implied a commitment to equality. Northerners had long ago perfected the practice of granting the abstractions of legal protection while denying social and political equality. This did not stop as black men entered the Union armies. African Americans who read black enlistment as a shift of their status in American society quickly learned otherwise as federal administrators formulated policies that confirmed patterns of invidious racial distinction.

Systematic inequity faced by black troops in the Union ranks encompassed all aspects of their terms of service. Every injustice, whether stemming from explicit policy or irregular enforcement, proved the lie to the breezy assurances of federal officials that those who fought under the American flag were assured its full protection and benefits. At least two policies, however, merit brief mention for the broader implications they suggest. The government's refusal to commission black officers demonstrated that the racial animus that had initially barred black enlistment not only persisted but had hardened, and its unwillingness to pay black soldiers at the same rate as whites showed that even as the apparatus of slavery was being dismantled, the Republic was devising alternate, less visible strategies to maintain the subordinate position of African Americans. Both policies provided common cause among black soldiers and sparked vigorous protest.

There is a world of difference between a commissioned and a noncommissioned officer. Commissioned officers, from lieutenant up, assume an elevated position above all enlisted men; they are recognized as "gentlemen" and can command units other than their own. Noncommissioned officers (sergeants and corporals), on the other hand, remain within the ranks, and their authority does not extend much beyond the regiment. Proponents of black enlistment claimed the right of black men to hold positions of command as a reward for commendable service. Racially motivated doubts about the ability of black men to lead in combat situations compounded by discomfort at the prospect of having blacks outrank whites prompted policy makers to take a decidedly different view. While the appointment of black men as noncommissioned officers was readily granted, the commis-

James Roberts, *Drummer*

sioning of black line officers met stiff resistance. With the brief exception of the Louisiana Native Guards, U.S. military policy pointedly prohibited the appointment of black commissioned officers.

War Department objections to black line officers did not extend in the same way to black chaplains and surgeons largely because these officers stood outside the regimental command structure. The few black men who obtained commissions to these ranks, however, remained vulnerable to prejudicial perceptions within the military. Chaplains had to be elected by regimental officers, thus making them subject to the bias of white officers. Black surgeons, because they could outrank other army physicians, white as well as black, stood vulnerable to the hostility of white officers and especially white surgeons. Very few chaplains and even fewer surgeons were offered commissions in the Union armies. Yet with these few appointments the War Department hoped to defuse criticism about the absence of black commissioned officers without threatening the white officer corps.

By 1865, in response to sustained protest and the undeniable success of black soldiers in the field, several prominent northern politicians were persuaded to support the commissioning of black officers. As the war was ending, a handful of black soldiers were awarded commissions. Even in this, however, the War Department hedged its bets by awarding these, almost without exception, after the war had ended and as the regiments with officers who would be awarded commissions were being mustered out of service.

When, on 25 August 1862, Secretary of War Edwin M. Stanton authorized Brigadier General Rufus B. Saxton, stationed in the Department of the South, to recruit the first "volunteers of African Descent," he provided that the men would, "receive the same pay and

Colored enlisted Men – Pay

What pay & rations ought colored enlisted men to receive under the law?

Opinion

By the 11th Section of the act of July 17th
1862 entitled "an act to define the pay &
emoluments &c" the President was authorized
to employ as many persons of African descent as he should deem necessary & proper
for the suppression of this rebellion, and for that
purpose he was authorized to organize and
use them in such manner as he judged for
the public welfare.

No provision was specially made for their compensation in
act. By the 15th Section of the act of July 17 entitled "an act to am
the act calling forth the militia &c" it is provided that all pe
enrolled under that act (authorizing the raising of 100,000 vols for
and who should enlist as infantry under the provisions of section 3d
et should be entitled to receive his 1st months pay & $25.00 bounty upon
mustering of his company or regiment into the service of the U.S (see se

2nd All persons enrolled under that act were entitled to receive (by Se
the pay & rations now allowed by law to soldiers according to their resp
grades. Provided that persons of African descent who should be employ
under this law should receive $10. per month and one ration each
ay of which pay $3. might be paid in clothing.

By the act of March 3d 1863 cooks of African descent are entitle
receive for the full compensation $10. per month and one ration each pe
of which monthly pay may be in clothing.

It seems therefore that in accordance with the foregoing acts per
African descent, received into the service of the United States, as v
eers under said acts, are entitled to receive as pay & $10 per mo
and one ration daily, of which monthly pay $3. may
paid in clothing   (Signed) Wm Whiting
                            Sol. War Dept

rations as are allowed by law to volunteers in the service." Stanton made the same commitment verbally to John A. Andrew, governor of Massachusetts.

White privates and corporals in the federal army were paid $13 per month, plus a $3.50 clothing allowance, in addition to a bounty of one, two, and three hundred dollars for one-, two-, and three-year enlistments. Company sergeants earned $17 per month; first sergeants $20, and regimental sergeants $21 per month. While the South Carolina and Massachusetts regiments were being raised, Stanton requested a finding from William Whiting, Solicitor to the War Department, regarding the pay of black troops. Whiting determined that black soldiers were entitled to pay of $7 per month ($10 minus a $3 clothing allowance) and no bounty. Black soldiers, regardless of rank (chaplains, sergeants, privates) were to be paid this amount. Whiting based his findings on the Militia Act of 1862. But the pay provisions of the Militia Act applied to laborers, not soldiers. Even if viewed solely from a legalistic perspective, the War Department, adhered to Whiting's recommendation despite Stanton's earlier promise of equal pay, despite similar guarantees made by recruiters and generals on its behalf, and despite provisions in the Enrollment Act of 1863 which guaranteed pay for draftees on a par with volunteers (The Enrollment Act applied to blacks as well as to whites).

Discrimination in pay sparked massive protest among the soldiers. Those with the courage of their convictions stood on the principle of equality, but it cost them dearly. Many of these men had families and loved ones to support. As they watched their wives and children slide into poverty, and then sink to destitution, they knew that their spouses could not turn to external resources for assistance. "The wives of the men are, they say often refused [at] the alms house for their color," one USCT officer wrote, "and are reduced to degradation that drives the husbands almost crazy."

The Massachusetts regiments made it clear that their protest was about principle, not just money, by refusing to accept pay even when the balance of their salaries was met by special provision of the Massachusetts state legislature. The South Carolina regiments had drawn at least one payment at the regular volunteer rate before the lower pay policy was placed into effect. When Sergeant William

William Whiting. *No. 127.* War Department. 23 April 1863. *Loomis-Wilder Family Papers, Manuscripts and Archives, Yale University Libraries.*

Jacob Roulette, *Private*; Hiram Jarvis,
Private; Marshall Moore, *Private*

Walker of Company A, 3rd South Carolina, led his men in stacking
their arms and refusing to perform any more duty until the matter of
pay was settled, he was charged with mutiny and executed by firing
squad before his entire brigade.

As the protests by the Massachusetts and South Carolina regiments gained in intensity throughout the summer and fall of 1863,
they were joined by the men in the Michigan regiments. When the
men of Rhode Island's 14th Heavy Artillery also joined the protests,
that regiment's commander retaliated by court-martialing two dozen
noncommissioned officers and men and by imposing sentences of as
much as one year imprisonment at hard labor.

Congress finally acted in mid-June 1864 by authorizing equal
pay for black soldiers retroactive to 1 January 1864, and by allowing
troops who had been free as of 19 April 1861 to draw back pay retroactive to time of enlistment. This last provision was a slap in the face to
the many recruits who had either escaped slavery to enlist or who had
been freed by provisions in the Second Confiscation Act. Still another
year would pass, however before Congress recognized Stanton's initial
order of August 1862 and authorized equal pay for the South Carolina
regiments from date of enlistment.

By 1864 the Civil War had become a war of attrition. With
Confederate forces swept from the Mississippi Valley and large parts
of the Atlantic seaboard, the army's most pressing needs were for
troops to protect lengthening supply lines and garrison outposts
throughout the expanding occupied territory. But the excessive fatigue
duty (manual labor) to which black troops were routinely assigned,
had nothing to do with military necessity. "Where white and black
troops come together in the same command," Brigadier General
Lorenzo Thomas noted matter-of-factly, "the latter have to do all the

work." It was the black troops who built earthworks and dug front-line trenches. Once they had made the fortifications secure, they were rotated out and a white regiment assumed its place in the line. Black troops laid out and policed the military camps, and they were assigned the most odious tasks within the camps. Through it all black soldiers were watched closely to see if they could measure up to military standards. Evaluations were generally based on the ability to drill smartly and perform effectively while on the march or in combat. Numerous officers complained that excessive fatigue detail siphoned off needed time for adequate drill. "Months have passed, at times," Brigadier General Daniel Ullman reported, "without the possibility of any drill at all."

Long days of fatigue lowered morale and wore out men's clothing. Their bedraggled appearance merely confirmed the belief that they were not fit to be soldiers. "Since the arrival of my command at this place on the 21st day of June, 1864," Lieutenant Colonel Branson of the 62nd USCT reported, "all men fit for duty not as camp guard or police have been worked eight to ten hours daily on the fortifications except Sunday, one day for review and half a day for muster and inspection. No white troops have been worked on these fortifications during said period except those held as prisoners and undergoing punishment."

Excessive fatigue duty also broke men's health. In October 1864, a medical review board found that more than a third of the enlistees in three black Missouri regiments had perished since enlistment. None of the fatalities were combat related. In combat situations a regiment that had lost one third of its fighting capacity would have been considered hard hit. For the black troops such losses were simply the price of enlistment.

Though assigned pride of place in the upcoming Battle of the Crater, the Fourth Division was not relieved of its other duties to prepare for this mission. Instead, its service record for July speaks plainly of the low regard in which these troops were held by senior commanders in the Army of the Potomac. Nominally assigned to the Ninth Corps, the Fourth Division was shuttled on detached service between the Second and Fifth Corps during the early weeks of July. While their superiors changed, the assignments given the men—digging ditches and building forts—remained the same. Indeed, the levies for work parties on the command were so great that on two occasions in mid-July General Ferrero registered formal complaints with his superiors. Captain R. K. Beecham, in the 23rd USCT (second brigade) later recalled, "I am prepared to say from actual knowledge

Adjutant General's Office,

Washington, D. C.,

July 14th, 1864.

Sir:

I have the honor to inform you that the date of muster into service of C. G. G. Merrill as a Surgeon in the Twenty Second Reg't of U. S. C. Troops Volunteers, made by Lieut. Hildeburn U. S. A. Commissary of Musters, _____ for _____, is changed from January 16th, 1864, to January 13th, 1864.

I am, sir, very respectfully,

Your obed't servant,

F. M. Taggard

Assistant Adjutant General.

(32)

To Cmdg Officer
22nd Reg. U. S. C. Troops
Near Petersburg Va.

---

derived from personal experience with the Fourth Division that the only duty assigned to the said division for more than a month before the battle of the Mine was work upon our trenches and fortifications. The Fourth Division during all that time was drilled especially in the use of pick and shovel, and in no other manner."

"The little regard which army surgeons have for human life and human suffering is dreadful to behold," Charles Merrill (Yale 1861, M.D. 1863) wrote to his father from Army Hospital No. 8 in Nashville, Tennessee, 11 February 1863. "A surgeon told me today that he had lost two or three cases, in his opinion, because he did not look out for certain accidents which are of common occurrence in practice and which every surgeon ought to look out for. He spoke of it with the greatest nonchalance as though it was of no consequence whatever." The sickness, disease and medical malfeasance to which Union soldiers were vulnerable was catastrophic for the men serving in the USCT units. Among white regiments, nearly two soldiers died of disease for every one who was killed or mortally wounded in battle; for black troops, the ratio was roughly ten to one. Approximately one in twelve white soldiers died of disease compared with one in five for the black troops.

While there is no explanation for such wanton wastage of human life, a few contributing factors can be identified: In the rush to meet national recruitment quotas without depleting the white northern labor force, black men in poor physical condition or who would otherwise have been disqualified, were often pressed into service. Few black men had had prior exposure, and therefore had no immunity, to the diseases that ravaged army camps. Adopting the spurious claim that black men had "natural" immunity to tropical diseases, military commanders withdrew white troops and disproportionately posted black troops to locations in lowland and subtropical climates where disease was rampant. The heavy fatigue duty to which the black troops were assigned often weakened and sometimes broke their health.

Furthermore, the haste with which many USCT regiments were organized outstripped the army's ability to find competent medical personnel. And not everyone was willing to accept an appointment with a black regiment. By the time the army finally began accepting black recruits, many of the best surgeons had already received earlier appointments and were no longer available. Since medical personnel in combat situations treated those brought to them regardless of unit, the army was loathe to appoint black surgeons, even to the USCT units, reasoning that the care they could provide would cause the greater discomfort to wounded and dying white soldiers. Dr. Alexander T. Augusta was typical of the at least eight black doctors who served as surgeons in the Union armies. Educated in Canada, Dr. Augusta's credentials were well above those of many army physicians, yet he spent most of the war on detached service, at a rendezvous camp for black troops, rather than with his regiment.

"Very few surgeons will do precisely the same for blacks as they would for whites," one USCT surgeon noted carefully. But behind the doctor's delicate phrasing lay the more brutal truth that for the black troops prejudice was a fact of life. Few USCT regiments had the full complement of regimental medical officers: one surgeon and two assistant surgeons. In response to unmet staffing needs, hospital stewards—recuperating patients who had demonstrated intelligence and could handle light duties—were appointed as assistant surgeons in black regiments, a practice that subjected black soldiers to the experiments and blunders of men who had no medical training or experience. Too many stories echo those of the soldier wounded during the Battle of Nashville (December 1864) who, one month after the engagement, lay in the filth of Hospital No. 16 with a leg wound that required amputation, his clothes having been unchanged since his admittance.

Horrified by the thought that in combat situations they and their men could be exposed to treatment by USCT medical personnel, officers in white regiments raised protests that the army could not ignore. In response, the military targeted some medical schools and combed the ranks of its contract physicians for candidates for the U.S. Colored Troops. It was most likely as a result of this latter effort that Charles Merrill came to serve with the USCT.

Immediately following his graduation from what was then the Medical Institution of Yale College, Dr. Merrill signed a contract with the army and was posted to Nashville, Tennessee. He was hoping for an appointment in one of the Ohio regiments. When this failed to materialize, Merrill found his opportunity with the 22nd USCT. As a surgeon, Merrill brought the same ambition that had distinguished his academic career to his responsibilities with the regiment. His letters to his father reveal a human concern for the health of the soldiers and show the pride he took in his ability to do good work. They also convey a sense of immediacy. Merrill wrote regularly and often, even when on the march or during heavy engagements. He found time to write on 3 April 1865 when the regiment entered Richmond as part of the Union vanguard. And he wrote later that month from Washington D.C. on the day that the 22nd served as part of the honor guard in Lincoln's funeral procession.

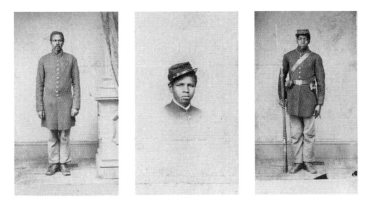

John Veach, *Fifer*; George Olden, *Drummer*, Co. D, 108th USCT; Jacob Weathers, *Private*

No mention is made in contemporary accounts about the arms shouldered by the Fourth Division in this battle. Whether these troops were armed with Spencer Repeating Rifles (one of the best) or Springfield smooth-bore muskets (among the worst), it is worth noting that, as a matter of course, troops serving in the USCT units were poorly armed.

"General," Brigadier General Edward Hinks wrote, appealing directly to the commander of the Department of Virginia and North Carolina,

> In view of the approaching campaign, and more especially on account of the recent inhumanities of the enemy perpetrated upon troops of like character to those of my command, I deem it my duty to urge that these troops shall be more efficiently armed, to enable them to defend themselves and lessen their liability to capture.
>
> There certainly out (sic) to be no objection to arming these troops with as effective a weapon as any that are placed in the hands of white Soldiers, who are to go into battle with none of the peculiar disadvantages to which my men will be Subject
>
> The present arms of several regiments in the division are inferior, in kind and manufacture.
>
> The Springfield Rifled musket of the Bridesburg manufacture is an unreliable gun. The contract Enfield Rifle is also unreliable, and one Reg't is armed with the Old Harpers Ferry smoothbore.[4]

As Hink's letter shows, it was not uncommon for USCT regiments within the same brigade to be assigned weapons of different make and model, each firing its own caliber of ammunition. This lack of uniformity in armaments not only hampered combat efficiency; in

The war news for a day or two past has not raised my spirits much - but I am yet sanguine that the war will end in the freedom of the slave and in the elevation of the Colored man. If this result shall only come, I shall be content to spend the balance of my life in retiracy. Tell, Dear William that while I should have been glad to see him in some office connected with the war, I am glad that he has not gone as a private. The hardships of a private are painful to think of. You will have seen, that Massachusitts has done by her Colored Soldiers as I predicted it would do. The state will pay the men precisely as white soldiers are paid - and let the old

people at Washington do as
they please about wiping
out their reproach. I do not
doubt however, that Congress
will at once do the honorable
thing about the pay, if it does
not about promotion.
Congress was the first to respect
the claims of justice and obey
the instinctive judgement
of the people, in fixing the
brand of its reprobation upon
slavehunting in shoulder
straps. And my belief is that
that body will show progress
at its present meeting.
Large bodies move slow —
but they move — and sometimes
move for more swiftly than
we give them credit for.
We have recently had a lecture
here from Miss Anna Dickenson,
She spoke wonderfully well

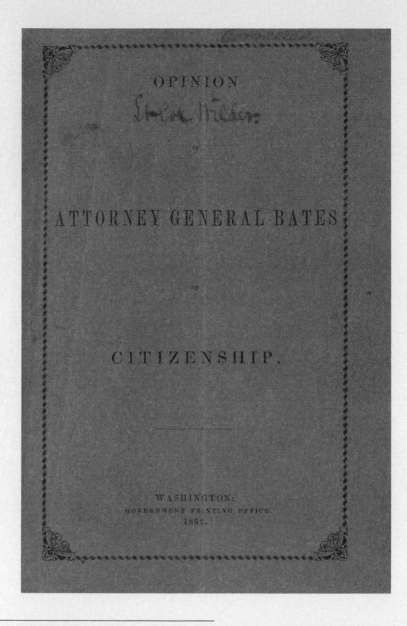

OPINION

OF

ATTORNEY GENERAL BATES

ON

CITIZENSHIP.

WASHINGTON:
GOVERNMENT PRINTING OFFICE.
1862.

Edward Bates. *Opinion of Attorney
General Bates on Citizenship.*
Washington: Government Printing
Office, 1862. *Loomis-Wilder Family
Papers, Manuscripts and Archives, Yale
University Libraries.*

combat situations, it could prove disastrous. General acceptance of the fact that black troops shouldered inferior arms is shown by the off-hand remark of another general, who after inspecting a regiment in New Orleans noted that it, "like the other Colored Troops, is armed with the old flinklock musket altered to percussion, turned in by the white volunteers and some of them twice condemned." Forty percent of the men of the 107th USCT, also in the line at Petersburg, were found to be armed with rifled muskets that had a defective main spring and could not fire.

Black troops fighting in the Civil War occupied a highly ambiguous position with regard to citizenship. Throughout the early 19th century, United States Attorneys General regularly concurred that the Constitution did not confer the rights and privileges of citizenship to African Americans. Black Americans were barred, by Congressional legislation, from handling the mails for fear that, among several reasons put forward by Postmaster General Gideon Granger in 1802, they would be able to mix with other people and learn, "that a man's rights do not depend on his color." The State Department, with few exceptions, denied the passport applications of black Americans.

Congress weighed in directly on the question of African American citizenship in the legislative debates leading up the Missouri Compromise. Hoping for acceptance as part of the United States, Missouri submitted its proposed constitution for Congressional approval in November 1820. The constitution sanctioned slavery, a provision that would have passed without objection, but it also enjoined the state legislature to pass laws "to prevent free negroes and mulattoes from coming to and settling in this state, under any pretext whatsoever." Secretary of State John Quincy Adams, among many others, considered this provision irreconcilable with a federal guarantee that "the citizens of each state shall be entitled to all privileges and immunities of citizens of the several states." Acceptance of Missouri's constitution as written would alter the terms of the U.S. Constitution and jeopardize whatever remnant of rights or status freedmen had. In March 1821 Congress voted to admit Missouri with a vague qualification disputing the "free Negro" clause. The Missouri legislature accepted this provision, then promptly enacted legislation that rendered it ineffective.

Any lingering doubts concerning the legal status of African Americans were dispelled by the Supreme Court's ruling in *Scott v. Sanford* (1857). Writing for the majority, Chief Justice Roger B. Taney concluded that African Americans had no rights "which white men are bound to respect."

While it served as the law of the land *Scott v. Sanford* was not without controversy. When the schooner *Elizabeth and Margaret* was detained in 1862 by the revenue cutter *Tiger* at South Amboy, New Jersey, because she was commanded by a "colored man," the Secretary of the Treasury seized the opportunity to address a formal inquiry regarding the citizenship of African Americans to Attorney General Edward A. Bates. "As colored masters are numerous in our coasting trade," the secretary wrote, "I submit, for your opinion ... *Are colored men citizens* of the United States, and therefore competent to command American vessels?" Since the acts regulating foreign and coastal trade limited the command of vessels to American citizens, the prominence of black seamen during the expansion of the American maritime industry in the first half of the nineteenth century had forced the issue on more than one occasion. Forty years earlier a similar question had been put to Attorney General William Wirt. In 1821 Wirt had ruled that black men were not citizens.⁵ On this occasion, Attorney General Bates replied with a lengthy opinion in which he concluded that "the *free man of color* ... if born in the United States, is a citizen of the United States." The Attorney General could not overrule the Supreme Court. *Scott v. Sanford* still held. But Bates's opinion would be confirmed by Congress six years later with passage of the Fourteenth Amendment.

If the black troops who placed themselves in harm's way encountered the enemy most frequently in the Union ranks, they faced an equally implacable foe when they took their places in the front lines. Historically, the greatest fear of southern slave owners had been the threat of insurrection. That fear was realized, in its fullest sense, as armed black troops marched into and throughout the South. Absent any official policy, Confederate officers debated whether captured black soldiers should be hanged or shot. Then in December 1862, Jefferson Davis, feigning due process, ordered that captured black soldiers be turned over to state authorities to be dealt with according to the appropriate state statutes. Every state in the Confederacy had laws on the books prescribing execution of black insurrectionists, usually by hanging.

By 1863, as unanswered Confederate threats began to jeopardize the recruitment process, federal policy makers realized that they could no longer remain silent. In July 1863, President Lincoln issued a proclamation vowing that, "for every soldier of the United States killed in violation of the laws of war, a rebel soldier shall be executed; and for every one enslaved by the enemy or sold into slavery, a rebel soldier shall be placed at hard labor on the public works, and continued at such labor until the other shall be released and receive the treatment due to a prisoner of war."

Confederate practice in the field may not always have been as extreme as the directives streaming out of Richmond, but the official policy encouraged abuse. Black troops taken prisoner were frequently sold into slavery or set to work building Confederate fortifications— both violations of the conventions of warfare. Rather than redressing atrocities as they discovered them, Union officers relayed these to their superiors. As the War Department queried its counterpart in the Confederacy about the validity of various claims, any sense of immediacy or horror faded. Even in the face of incontrovertible proof that hundreds of black soldiers had been slaughtered after surrendering at Fort Pillow (12 April 1864), the federal government found it more convenient to engage in fact-finding than to take action.

In his initial report, General Nathan Bedford Forrest, leader of the Confederate force during the Fort Pillow engagement gloated, "The river was dyed with the blood of the slaughtered for 200 yards." But the wave of indignation that swept the nation following reports of the massacre embarrassed the Confederacy. Hoping not to alienate European public opinion at a time when they still hoped for French or British intervention in their favor, Confederate policy makers urged their officers not to publicize the executions of black soldiers taken in the field. The officers obliged, and the patterns of abuse continued. Although the federal government did halt prisoner exchanges with the Confederacy late in the war when the South excluded black soldiers from their prisoner lists, the Lincoln administration never saw the need to fulfill the president's pledge to avenge the murder and enslavement of black soldiers. "The Black Flag order of the Confederacy [i.e. policy on the execution of prisoners] was a godsend for the colored regiments," recalled the commander of the 2nd Kansas (Colored) Volunteer Infantry. "Every officer and every soldier knew that it meant the bayonet, with no quarter, whenever and wherever they met the enemy."

Despite, or perhaps more properly, because of the virtually unassailable challenges at every side, many of the black men who enlisted in the Union armies were highly motivated. They may have worn the same uniform and marched under the same flag as white northern soldiers, but the black troops fought a completely different war. The liberation they sought encompassed far more than freedom from chattel slavery. The lessons of their enlistment had shown just how hollow every seeming advance of their civil rights would be if motivated by political necessity or convenience. Northern hostility

Henry Price, *Private*; James Rowlett,
Private, Company barber and fiddler;
Emmit Adams, *Private, Company clerk*

made it clear that nothing would be given to them. Whatever degree of social and political participation African Americans hoped to achieve in the body politic would have to come through reliance on their resources alone. Recognizing that judges and politicians generally follow, rather than shape, public opinion, it was to the court of public opinion that they took their cause. The fact that nationhood itself was threatened by a difference in opinion over whether African Americans could be claimed as property or acknowledged, however rhetorically, as human beings, showed just how precarious their position was. These men fought because they had to. The risks were high, too high really, but so too were the potential rewards. The Battle of the Crater, and more broadly the experiences of black troops in the Civil War, showed in human terms just what was at stake.

+   +   +   +   +

While they did not know it then, things had begun to unravel for the men of the Fourth Division on 28 July when Major General Ambrose Burnside rode over to the headquarters of Major General George C. Meade, commander of the Army of the Potomac, to inform him that the mine was ready. There Burnside was informed that his plan to have black troops lead his advance had been rejected. Meade also insisted that the first troops over the Union breastworks advance directly to Cemetery Hill rather than protect the Union flanks as Burnside had intended. When Burnside stuck to his guns on both points, Meade promised to lay the whole matter before Lieutenant General Ulysses S. Grant, general in chief of the Union armies.

The following day, while meeting with the commanders of his three white divisions, Burnside was informed that Grant had endorsed

Meade's decision: the black troops were not to lead the attack. When each of the three division commanders present argued why his men could not lead the assault, a frustrated Burnside finally had his generals "pull straws" to determine who would accept the assignment. The lot fell to Brigadier General James A. Ledlie, commander of the First Division. With barely twelve hours left before the mine was set to explode, Burnside and his commanders hastily revised their strategy. It was decided that the First Division would advance directly to Cemetery Hill. The Third would follow and form a defensive line to the left at the breach; the Second would do likewise on the right.

The only division commander not present at this meeting was Edward Ferrero, commander of the Fourth Division. Having failed for the second time to receive Senate confirmation for his appointment to brigadier general, Ferrero—knowing that his division was assigned to lead the attack and with no definite return date—had left abruptly on 21 July to personally plead his case in Washington. Although he returned and resumed command of the division on the 29th at 7 p.m., none of the Fourth Division's brigade or regimental commanders learned of the change in strategy until the early morning hours of 30 July.

The mine's explosion was delayed by a faulty fuse. At a time officially reckoned as "sixteen minutes before five," four tons of gunpowder exploded beneath Elliott's Salient creating a gaping crater 30 feet deep, 60 feet wide, and 170 feet long. After initially retreating before the mine blast, the lead brigade of the First Division crossed the open ground to the smoldering crater. Instead of pressing on and seizing Cemetery Hill, however, these men stopped at the crater to view the devastation and began mopping up the carnage. They also sought shelter from the increasingly spiteful Confederate counterfire. Hard on their heels the division's second brigade also stopped at the crater. As the men of the two brigades intermingled, regimental and company organization disintegrated. Efforts to straighten out the mess merely compounded the confusion. "Every officer from colonel down to second lieutenant was giving orders of some kind, most of them being contradictory," a Massachusetts captain remembered.

As the Third and Second Divisions pressed dutifully forward, the scene at the crater disintegrated into complete chaos. Officers lost control of their units. With no one of sufficient rank on the scene to revise the initial strategy in response to the changing situation in the field, the Union assault became paralyzed. Meanwhile Confederate reinforcements converged at the threatening breakthrough. The federals' failure to roll up the enemy's lines on either flank exposed them to volleys of musketry from the rebel trenches. A Confederate battery, wheeled hastily into position, swept the area with shrapnel and canister. Ninety minutes after the initial advance and with three quarters of the Ninth Corps (over 10,000 men) committed, Burnside's strategy lay a complete shambles.

The Fourth Division now stood poised to advance the 100 yards across no-man's-land to the crater. Lieutenant Colonel Charles Loring, the corps' inspector general, had been watching events unfold all morning. Loring was so disturbed by the thought of additional troops being committed to the debacle that he countermanded their orders to advance, then raced in search of Burnside. Committing additional men to the engagement, Loring argued, would yield no added benefit. Far better to deploy those men already at the crater in cleaning out the network of traverses and bombproofs that lay between it and the Jerusalem Plank Road. But Burnside, responding to similar orders from Meade, remained adamant: the Fourth was to advance "at all hazards."

Confederate artillery shells now ranged the jump-off point, making it nearly impossible for the black troops to advance in an orderly fashion. "The appearance of the regimental colors seemed to be a signal to the enemy's batteries," recalled Colonel Delevan Bates of the 30th, "and it was volley after volley of canister and shrapnel they gave us." "Down went our flag," wrote Lieutenant F. S. Bowley of the same regiment, "the color sergeant staining the stars and stripes with his blood." Bates tried to lead his men around the salient, but a withering Confederate fire forced his lead column into the smoking pit. Lieutenant Colonel H. Seymour Hall chose a different route. Leading the 43rd along the sheltered edge of an enemy entrenchment, Hall ordered a charge that plunged his men into hand-to-hand combat with the enemy. In the day's fighting the 43rd would take 200 Confederate prisoners, capture a stand of Confederate colors, and recapture the regimental colors of one of the white units that had been lost earlier in the day.

As what remained of the four regiments of the first brigade linked up on the opposite side of the crater, the second brigade, led by the 31st USCT, made its deadly passage across no-man's land.[6] A few of the white units, shamed by the Fourth's advance, fell into line and moved forward as the second brigade forced its way through the crater vortex; others, loudly proclaiming that they "would never follow 'niggers' or be caught in their company" remained as they were.

The first brigade, meanwhile, had begun the grim task of clearing out the trenches directly blocking its advance. "The enemy's works on this part of the line was a perfect honeycomb of bomb

Solomon Starks, *Private*

proofs, trenches, covered ways, sleeping holes, and little alleys running in every direction," Bates recalled, "and in each hole there appeared one or more rebel soldiers, some ready to 'kill the niggers' when they came in view and some praying for mercy."

The one officer not present to witness any part of the fighting was General Ferrero. After giving the order to advance, Ferrero had retired to an aid station well behind Union lines where he remained throughout the engagement. His principal contribution seems to have been an order he sent forward through an aide to Colonels Sigfried and Thomas telling them that their original orders remained in effect: press on to the Jerusalem Plank Road and seize Cemetery Hill.

Somehow, the two brigades of the Fourth Division managed to do what the men of the First Division had not. In the face of concentrated fire from Confederate reinforcements at their front and harassed by fusillades from their exposed flanks in the rear, the men of the first and second brigades reformed their ranks and—joined by units from Colonel Zenas Bliss's and Colonel Simon Griffith's brigades—advanced towards the Jerusalem Plank Road.

In yet another of the signal failures retarding Union efforts that day, the Fifth Corps, supporting the Ninth on its right, failed to mount enough pressure to prevent the Confederates from withdrawing reinforcements for their counter attacks at the crater later that day. Early on in the engagement, Major General Robert B. Potter, commanding the Second Division (Ninth Corps), had sent a dispatch to Burnside urging that diversionary action be taken at some other point along the line to lessen the Confederate concentration at the crater. Potter never received a reply. In testimony before Congress, Major General Gouverneur K. Warren, commander of the Fifth Corps, said that he had not received orders to attack the enemy along his part of the line and had not done so. The larger Union strategy called for the Fifth and Eighteenth Corps to follow the Ninth through the breach at the crater and on into Petersburg. With the breach never secured, the Fifth remained inactive throughout the engagement.

Brigadier General William Mahone C.S.A. commanded the Confederate force opposite the Union Fifth Corps about a mile southwest of the crater. Sizing up the situation quickly, Mahone withdrew three brigades from the five he commanded and marched them double-quick towards the Union thrust. Mahone was a former Petersburg railroad executive, and his men were highly motivated. Some had been recruited right there in Petersburg; all were inflamed by grapevine rumors that the advancing black troops were giving no quarter.

The Fourth Division, and those units fighting with them, advanced about 200 yards beyond the crater, just under half the dis-

Stereograph. Tombstone. Unknown
U.S. Colored Soldier. Arlington
National Cemetery.

tance to the Jerusalem Plank Road. There a Confederate counterattack drove them back. Lieutenant Bowley watched in horror as the federal line bent and then shattered: "For a moment the men moved backward, to the left, firing as they retreated; then the enemy charged with a yell, and poured a volley into their very faces," Bowley recalled. "Instantly the whole body broke, went over the breastworks toward the Union line, or ran down the trenches towards the crater."

By mid-morning all that remained of the Union assault was about a thousand disorganized men, both black and white, trapped in and around the crater. For these men the situation quickly deteriorated from one of combat to something far worse. The day was intensely hot, and the men had been without food or drink since the previous night. The suffering of the wounded was acute. Moreover, while consolidating their forces, the Confederates had brought up a squad of light mortar. As these found their range, dismembered bodies began

to litter the pit in all directions. Those who tried to escape across no-man's land were mercilessly cut down by an enemy that now surrounded them on three sides. Opting to wait until nightfall, Burnside steadfastly refused to withdraw his troops, fearing that to do so before then would cause widespread panic behind Union lines.

The black troops knew that if captured they faced an uncertain fate. Now, in gruesome counterpoint to the draft riots of a year earlier, the racism within the Union ranks revealed itself in a new and terrible way. "It was believed among the whites," wrote George Kilmer, 14th New York Heavy Artillery (Ledlie's First Division), "that the enemy would give no quarter to the negroes, or to the whites taken with them.... It has been positively asserted that white men bayoneted blacks who fell back into the crater. This was in order to preserve the whites from Confederate vengeance. Men boasted in my presence that blacks had thus been disposed of, particularly when the Confederates came up."

At "one o'clock by the watch" one survivor recalled, the rebels made their final assault. The fighting was chaotic and violent. "We say slaughter," said John W. Pratt of the 30th USCT, "for we can call it nothing else—nor can any one who was present say truthfully that it was not." A veteran of Sanders's Alabama brigade, "Gen. Mahone had told the soldiers of the brigade that negro troops were in possession of the Crater and had come in yelling 'No quarter for the Rebels!' He did not say 'Show no quarter!' but Sander's men decided that point."

The wanton killing of men who had thrown aside their weapons and sought to surrender—and those, who seeing that surrender was futile, fought on to the death—beggars description. "Within ... ten minutes," according to one Virginia soldier, "the whole floor of the trench was strewn with the dead bodies of negroes, in some places in such numbers that it was difficult to make one's way along the trench without stepping on them." Much of the fighting was done at close quarters; it was hand-to-hand, bayonet and musket-butts. "How the negroe's skulls cracked with the blows," one North Carolina soldier chortled. Writing home a week after the battle, a Georgia man regretfully acknowledged, "some four negroes went to the rear as we could not kill them as fast as they passed us."

By mid-afternoon, the Confederates had regained possession of the crater. Those black troops who had somehow managed to survive and be taken prisoner watched as many, though not all, of their officers tore the insignia from their uniforms and denied any association with them.

Lewis Chapman, *Private*; George
Grigsby, *Private*; George Brown, *Private*

+ + + + +

"A sad day for our corps," a New Hampshire diarist ended his 31 July
entry. "The old story again—a big slaughter and nothing gained."
The careless squander of what had promised to be sure success, and
the horrific loss of life without tangible benefit, magnified the tragedy
of the crater. "So fair an opportunity," Grant later testified, "will prob-
ably never occur again for carrying fortifications; preparations were
good, orders ample, and everything so far as I can see, subsequent to
the explosion of the mine, shows that almost without loss the crest
beyond the mine could have been carried." Union failure in the
engagement meant that the siege of Petersburg, with much suffering
to both sides, dragged on for another eight months. When Petersburg
fell 3 April 1865, federal troops entered Richmond the same day. Less
than one week later, Lee surrendered.

But while they would share the continuing hardships of the
ongoing siege and war, and as their dead lay among the "slaughter[ed],"
the Battle of the Crater held a special resonance for the men of the
Fourth Division. For these men, the ideological implications of their
enlistment, the endless second-guessing of their capabilities, and the
limited opportunities to visibly demonstrate their ability in frontline
engagements charged each brush, battle, and skirmish in ways that
encompassed more than military significance.

Meade later explained his refusal to allow the black troops to
lead the attack by characterizing the battle as, "an operation which I
knew beforehand was one requiring the best troops...." This, of
course, had been Burnside's reasoning: the men of the Fourth
Division were the freshest, and judging by their advance, the most
highly motivated troops in his command. Meade, for his own reasons,
countermanded that strategy.

Cartes de visite. Obverse (left) and reverse (right) of the regimental color of the 6th United States Colored Troops. The flag was presented by the citizens of Philadelphia. Its artwork is attributed to David Bustill Bowser of Philadelphia. The motto, "Freedom for All." The flag was rescued by Sergeant Major Thomas R. Hawkins during the engagement at Deep Bottom, Virginia, 21 July 1864. Five years after the war, Sergeant Hawkins was awarded the Medal of Honor for his valor.

In the wave of shame and frustration that swept the Union ranks following the defeat everyone, it seemed, blamed the black troops for the failed outcome. Rumor spread quickly. "[A]t Petersburg, they have had a stunner, and would have done something if it hadn't been for the nigger troops," a cavalryman serving north of the James wrote a friend in early August, "but it was too warm for them and they took the backtrack, leaving a gap open and the Johnnies rushed in and the troops that was on the right and left of it had to fall back to keep from being flanked, you see." Opinions were no more charitable closer to home. "I say put the niggers out of the corps as I do not want to be in the corps they are," a Ninth volunteer heatedly declared.

Those from the Fourth who knew better than to judge themselves by white standards also understood that those judgments had serious implications. Not just the record, but the perceptions of their performance hardened opinion in ways that no amount of blood could wash away. Those perceptions influenced commanders' discretion in handing out assignments, and it informed the scope of potential opportunity for USCT units in the federal service. As accusations flew throughout the corps and the Union armies, the men of the Fourth Division bore witness to their experience through silence.

"Until we fought the battle of the crater," Colonel Thomas later said of the men, "they sang ["Like Men of War"] every night to the exclusion of all other songs. After that defeat they sang it no more."

The Fourth Division, in keeping with a general pattern among the USCT units, suffered far heavier casualties than any of the other three divisions in the Ninth Corps—this despite the preponderance of white soldiers in the engagement and the fact that the Fourth had entered the battle a full ninety minutes after the other three divisions. Official tallies list 209 killed or mortally wounded from the Fourth Division, compared with 227 from the First, Second, and Third Divisions combined. After carefully examining pension files and compiled service records, at least one Civil War historian has identified an additional 227 men from among those listed as missing from the Fourth as having been killed either during the fighting or immediately afterwards.7 Of the four Medals of Honor awarded to the men of the division Sergeant Decatur Dorsey of the 39th USCT was the one black soldier so acknowledged for his valor. His citation reads, "Planted his colors on the Confederate works in advance of his regiment, and when the regiment was driven back to the Union works he carried the colors there and bravely rallied the men."

Once the war ended, white regiments were quickly mustered

Bob Fore, *Private*; Jacob Staniford, *Private*

out of service in response to clamors by northern white communities that the men be brought home. Black troops were kept in the field to police the peace—and for other more paternalistic reasons. But their presence throughout the South was a potent reminder of the social changes taking place. Southerners complained bitterly to the officers of the USCT units, their politicians, and federal government officials about the presence of black troops in and near their cities and towns. The hatred that the black troops' presence inflamed among indignant whites sparked numerous incidents of violence between white citizens and the soldiers. Instead of utilizing the troubled situation to demonstrate that fundamental change was afoot, the army, like the North in general, moved to placate wounded southern pride at the black troops' expense. While Texas, in 1865, was not without strategic significance, it was the army's willingness to view black troops as the cause of the conflicts in the South and a corresponding desire to get them out of the way quickly that resulted in the posting of most of the USCT units to the brutal Texas frontier in the summer of 1865. There excessive fatigue duty, sickness and disease extracted a fearful toll.

Surgeon Merrill, still with the 22nd, wrote to his father from Brownsville, Texas, 2 July 1865. "You can have no idea of our desperate situation," Merrill wrote. "I never saw such a thing done before. The idea of putting ten thousand men in such a country without using any provision—or making any provision is more than preposterous. It is damnable.... I do not want to see my men murdered by inches, when there is no necessity for any such thing." Merrill was mustered out of service along with his regiment on 16 October 1865. The last of the USCT regiments—the 124th USCT—left the rolls on 20 December 1867.

+ + + + +

Roughly 187,000 black soldiers and 29,500 sailors served in the Union armies and navy during the Civil War. At best, these figures are approximations. Perhaps 135,000 of those who served had been former slaves. Of approximately 38,000 fatalities, roughly 2,870 were combat-related; most of the rest succumbed to disease. During the war, black troops participated in 449 engagements with Confederate forces. Sixteen black soldiers and four black sailors were awarded the newly minted Medal of Honor. In late July 1866, Congress passed an act authorizing the postwar military establishment of the United States. Ten cavalry regiments were authorized, "two of which shall be composed of colored men"—these became the 9th and 10th U.S. Cavalry. Twenty-seven regiments of infantry, four of which would be black units, were also authorized. These four were eventually collapsed to two, the 24th and 25th U.S. Infantry.

As the majority of black veterans returned home after the war, those who returned to southern and what had been border states were met with waves of violence from indignant whites eager to avenge Confederate defeat. No amount of evidence of gross injustice prompted government intervention. When, after months of investigation, General Clinton B. Fisk reported that black Kentucky veterans were "*scourged, beaten,* and *shot at* and driven from their families and homes...." the state legislature accused him of fabricating evidence.

The physical violence that black veterans were subject to was matched by other forms of cruelty. In the wave of Civil War nostalgia that swept the country during the latter half of the nineteenth century, the contributions of the black soldiers and the conditions under which they served were quietly omitted from the record. "[The] nation seems to be ashamed that [it] gave the slave a chance to strike a blow for himself," one veteran innocently observed in 1887. Barred from national discourse, these soldiers bore witness to a different Civil War than the one the nation chose to celebrate. For them the hostilities—"the late unpleasantness" as it was sometimes recalled—did not end with any military surrender. And perhaps this, finally, is the enduring lesson of their wartime example.

Whether in victory—Honey Springs (17 July 1863), Nashville (15–16 December 1864), Fort Fisher (February 1865)—or in defeat, the conditions under which black troops fought during the Civil War tempered their experiences in ways that do not show in official records. Engaging the enemy on two fronts, black troops contended with pervasive racism in the North while fighting to end slavery in the

South. The war introduced these men to worlds of experience far beyond the marginalized existence many had known as freemen and the repression others had suffered under slavery. Where opportunity, however circumscribed, presented itself, those with initiative acquired rudimentary education and developed skills in leadership. But the price they paid collectively can never be tabulated. The war shattered the bodies and psyches of some of these men. And it steeled the determination of others for the sterner tests that lay ahead.

Bethuel Hunter
New Haven, December 2003

Carte de visite. Unidentified soldiers.
These soldiers wear the dress uniforms
of sergeant majors, complete with non-
commissioned officers' sashes, swords,
and gauntlets. Sergeant major is the
highest ranking non-commissioned
officer in an infantry regiment.

1. The Army of the Potomac was divided into corps and then successively subdivided into divisions, brigades, regiments, and companies.

2. The Fourth Division was commanded by Brigadier General Edward Ferrero. *First Brigade:* Colonel Joshua K. Sigfried, commanding; Lieutenant Colonel Charles J. Wright, 27th USCT; Colonel Delevan Bates, 30th USCT; Colonel Ozora P. Stearns, 39th USCT; Lieutenant Colonel H. Seymour Hall, 43rd USCT. *Second Brigade:* Colonel Henry Goddard Thomas, commanding; Lieutenant Colonel Joseph G. Perkins, 19th USCT; Colonel Cleaveland J. Campbell, 23rd USCT; Lieutenant Colonel Charles S. Russell, 28th USCT; Lieutenant Colonel John A. Bross, 29th USCT; Lieutenant Colonel W. E. W. Ross, 31st USCT. The first brigade numbered 2,000 men; the second, 2,300.

3. Slavery was formally abolished in the United States with passage of the Thirteenth Amendment in December 1865.

4. Smooth-bore muskets were not only less accurate, they had one-fifth the range of rifled muskets.

5. Wirt's ruling applied to freemen in Virginia, but later interpretations extended its meaning considerably.

6. The 31st USCT consisted of the 30th Battalion Connecticut Volunteers along with troops from New York and Virginia. Two men from New Haven, both members of the 31st USCT, were killed in this battle. Captain Richard R. Woodruff, Company C was wounded and died 11 August. Sergeant Tilghmas S. Wood, Company C was killed. A third, private William D. Harmon, 31st USCT, Company C was listed as missing in action. Private Harmon was most likely killed. By the time the two sides had agreed to a truce to bury the dead and succor the wounded, the bodies of the fallen were so discolored and bloated that even race was indistinguishable but for the hair.

7. Noah Andre Trudeau, *Like Men of War.* (New York: Little, Brown and Company, 1998), 247.

For a lucid account of the engagements in which black troops fought during the Civil War see: Noah Andre Trudeau, *Like Men of War: Black Troops in the Civil War 1862-1865.* (New York, 1998). For a comprehensive study: Ira Berlin, Joseph P. Reidy, and Leslie S. Rowland, eds. *Freedom: A Documentary History of Emancipation, 1861-1867.* Series II. (New York, 1982). John David Smith, ed. *Black Soldiers in Blue: African American Troops in the Civil War Era.* (Chapel Hill, NC, 2002) provides excellent topical coverage. Additional secondary sources include: Dudley Taylor Cornish, *The Sable Arm: Black Troops in the Union Army, 1861-1865* (New York, 1956); Joseph T. Glatthaar, *Forged in Battle: The Civil War Alliance of Black Soldiers and White Officers.* (New York, 1990); Benjamin Quarles, *The Negro in the Civil War* (Boston, 1953). For accounts by black Civil War veterans: George W. Williams, *A History of the Negro Troops in the War of the Rebellion, 1861-1865.* (New York, 1888); Joseph T. Wilson, *The Black Phalanx: A History of the Negro Soldiers of the United States in the Wars of 1775-1812 and 1861-65.* (Hartford, 1888).

A CHECKLIST OF THE EXHIBITION

Frederick Douglass. Autograph note signed. 1859.

_____. *Life and Times of Frederick Douglass.* Boston: De Wolfe, Fiske & Co., 1893.

_____. Cartes de visite portraits.

_____. Autograph letter signed to an unidentified friend. 21 November, 1863.

J[ames] M[adison] Bell. "What Shall We Do with the Contrabands?" *Pacific Appeal.* 24 May, 1862.

Anonymous. Autograph letter to Edwin M. Stanton, Secretary of War. ca. 13 September, 1862. *Loomis-Wilder Family Papers, Manuscripts and Archives, Yale University Libraries.*

_____. Autograph document to General John A. Dix. 1 July, 1862. *Loomis-Wilder Family Papers, Manuscripts and Archives, Yale University Libraries.*

_____. Autograph letter to Judge Rolles. 13 September, 1862. *Loomis-Wilder Family Papers, Manuscripts and Archives, Yale University Libraries.*

James E. Yeatman. *A Report on the Condition of the Freedmen of Mississippi.* Saint Louis: Western Sanitary Commission Rooms, 1864.

Edward Bates. *Opinion of Attorney General Bates on Citizenship.* Washington: Government Printing Office, 1862. *Loomis-Wilder Family Papers, Manuscripts and Archives, Yale University Libraries.*

Recruitment broadside. U. S. Colored Troops, Philadelphia. *ca.* 1863.

E. D. Townsend. *General Orders No. 143.* Washington: War Department. 22 May, 1863. *Loomis-Wilder Family Papers, Manuscripts and Archives, Yale University Libraries.*

E. D. Townsend. *General Orders No. 144.* Washington: War Department. 22 May, 1863. *Loomis-Wilder Family Papers, Manuscripts and Archives, Yale University Libraries.*

L. Thomas. *Orders No. 7.* Vicksburg, Mississippi. 11 March, 1864.

Muster Rolls. Second United States Colored Infantry. 6 July, 1863. *Loomis-Wilder Family Papers, Manuscripts and Archives, Yale University Libraries.*

Theodore F. Wright. Sara A. Wright's Album. 22 March, 1865.

United States War Department. Map of the United States of America Showing the Boundaries of the Union and Confederate Geographical Divisions and Departments. 31 December, 1862.

Gold pen—and the original box for the pen—used by Abraham Lincoln to sign the Emancipation Proclamation. 1 January, 1863.

Muster Roll. Second United States Colored Infantry. 31 October, 1863. *Loomis-Wilder Family Papers, Manuscripts and Archives, Yale University Libraries.*

Autograph document signed. Colonel Benjamin R. Townsend. *Instructions for Making Muster and Pay Roll.* 28 February, 1864. *Loomis-Wilder Family Papers, Manuscripts and Archives, Yale University Libraries.*

William Whiting. Autograph opinion signed. *No. 127.* War Department. 23 April, 1863. *Loomis-Wilder Family Papers, Manuscripts and Archives, Yale University Libraries.*

Autograph document. *Inventory of effects of George Haughton.* 13 January, 1864. *Loomis-Wilder Family Papers, Manuscripts and Archives, Yale University Libraries.*

Autograph document. *Inventory of effects of Henry Gainer.* 5 April, 1864. *Loomis-Wilder Family Papers, Manuscripts and Archives, Yale University Libraries.*

J. E. Lockwood. Autograph document signed. Sworn statement by relation of deceased. Camp Stanton, Benedict, Maryland. 13 February, 1864. *Lewis Ledyard Weld Family Papers, Manuscripts and Archives, Yale University Libraries.*

O. E. Pratt. Autograph document signed. Receipt from sale of effects. Camp Stanton, Benedict, Maryland. 26 February, 1864. *Lewis Ledyard Weld Family Papers, Manuscripts and Archives, Yale University Libraries.*

Louis V. Caziarc. Document signed. *General Orders No. 132.* Headquarters, Department of the Gulf, New Orleans. 18 September, 1864. *Loomis-Wilder Family Papers, Manuscripts and Archives, Yale University Libraries.*

Captain John J. Barholf. Autograph document signed. *Inventory of the effects of Henry Hamilton.* 4 November, 1864. *Loomis-Wilder Family Papers, Manuscripts and Archives, Yale University Libraries.*

H. Crain. Autograph document signed. "Amount Fines Imposed by Provost Court of the Island of Key West." May 1865. *Loomis-Wilder Family Papers, Manuscripts and Archives, Yale University Libraries.*

A. H. Newton. *Out of the Briars: An Autobiography and Sketch of the Twenty-ninth Regiment Connecticut Volunteers.* 1910; rpt. Miami: Mnemosyne Publishing Co., 1969.

Edward P. Rogers. Autograph document signed. *List of Clothing Camp and Garrison Equipage.* 12 April, 1865.

Grand Army of the Republic. *A List of Those From New Haven, Conn. Who Lost Their Lives in the War of the Rebellion, 1861-1865.* 30 April, 1889.

Ernest Saunders. *Blacks in the Connecticut National Guard: A Pictorial and Chronological History: 1870-1919.* New Haven, Connecticut: New Haven Afro-American Historical Society, Inc., 1977.

Consider H. Willett. Autograph letter signed to E. R. Moore. 18 October, 1864. *Loomis-Wilder Family Papers, Manuscripts and Archives, Yale University Libraries.*

Officer's Commission. 9 February, 1863. *Loomis-Wilder Family Papers, Manuscripts and Archives, Yale University Libraries.*

Application, and death certificate of veteran Henry Moss (Private, Company H, 16th United States Colored Troops) to the Ohio Soldiers' and Sailors' Home.

F. M. Taggard. Document signed. Correcting commission date of Charles G. G. Merrill as Surgeon, 22nd United States Colored Troops. 14 July, 1864. *Charles G. G. Merrill Papers, Manuscripts and Archives, Yale University Libraries.*

Charles G. G. Merrill. Autograph letter signed to Annie. 16 June, 1864. *Charles G. G. Merrill Papers, Manuscripts and Archives, Yale University Libraries.*

_____. Autograph letter signed to father. 17 June, 1864. *Charles G. G. Merrill Papers, Manuscripts and Archives, Yale University Libraries.*

_____. Autograph letter signed to father. 23 June, 1864. *Charles G. G. Merrill Papers, Manuscripts and Archives, Yale University Libraries.*

_____. Autograph letter signed to father. 2 August, 1864. *Charles G. G. Merrill Papers, Manuscripts and Archives, Yale University Libraries.*

Photograph. Company E, 4th U. S. Colored Troops, Fort Lincoln, Virginia. *ca.* 1864.

Photograph. Private Charles R. Douglass, 54th Massachusetts Volunteers. *ca.* 1865.

Carte de visite. Double portrait, unidentified sergeant majors. *ca.* 1865.

Carte de visite. Unidentified veteran.

Carte de visite. Sentry shoulders musket at attention as soldiers, rifles stacked, relax before "A" tent. *ca.* 1865.

Cartes de visite. Obverse and reverse of the regimental colors of the 6th U. S. Colored Troops. *ca.* 1865.

Edwin M. Stanton. Secretary of War. Document signed. Captain's commission. 6 October, 1863. *Lewis Ledyard Weld Family Papers, Manuscripts and Archives, Yale University Libraries.*

William Birney. Autograph letter signed to "President of the Board of Examiners." 11 September, 1863. *Lewis Ledyard Weld Family Papers, Manuscripts and Archives, Yale University Libraries.*

Lewis Ledyard Weld. Autograph letter signed to mother. 17 August, 1864. *Lewis Ledyard Weld Family Papers, Manuscripts and Archives, Yale University Libraries.*

_____. Autograph letter signed to mother. 20 August, 1864. *Lewis Ledyard Weld Family Papers, Manuscripts and Archives, Yale University Libraries.*

_____. Autograph letter signed to Mason. 22 August, 1864. *Lewis Ledyard Weld Family Papers, Manuscripts and Archives, Yale University Libraries.*

Peter H. Clark. *The Black Brigade of Cincinnati: Being a Report of its Labors and a Muster-Roll of its Members together with Various Orders, Speeches, &c.* Cincinnati: Printed by Jos. B. Boyd, 1864.

Henry O'Reilly. *First Organization of Colored Troops in the State of New York, to aid in Suppressing the Slaveholder's Rebellion.* New York: Baker & Godwin, Printers, 1864.

Five stereographs: three of black federal troops in various parts of Virginia; two of army laborers.

Langston Hughes. "Portrait of a Woman: Harriet Tubman." Typescript draft of poem, n.d.

Charlotte L. Forten. *The Journal of Charlotte L. Forten.* Edited, with an introduction and notes, by Ray Allen Billington. New York: Dryden Publishers, 1953.

Susie King Taylor. *Reminiscences of my Life in Camp.* Boston: Published by the Author, 1902.

George W. Williams. *A History of the Negro Troops in the War of the Rebellion, 1861–1865.* New York: Harper & Brothers, 1888.

Joseph T. Wilson. *The Black Phalanx: A History of Negro Soldiers in the Wars of 1775-1812, 1861–65.* Hartford, Connecticut: American Publishing Company, 1888.

Tintype. Edward R. Richardson and his wife Fannie Sturgis. *ca.* 1865.

Real photographic postcard. Richardson as a veteran. *ca.* 1915.

Photograph. Company of black GAR veterans at Tomb of the Unknown Dead of the Civil War. *ca.* 1905.

Application, and death certificate of veteran Henry Moss to the Ohio Soldiers' and Sailors' Home.

Paul Laurence Dunbar. *Lyrics of Lowly Life.* New York: Dodd, Mead and Company, 1896.

Two of Douglass's three sons: Lewis Henry and Charles Redmond served in the 54th Massachusetts Regiment. Both men survived the war.

The "Decade Meeting" (referred to on page 1) was the thirteenth anniversary celebration of the American Anti-Slavery Society, held 3–4 December 1863 at Philadelphia's Concert Hall. With the Emancipation Proclamation having been issued in January, many of the Society's members, most notably William Lloyd Garrison its current president, considered its mission accomplished and hoped that this would be its final convention. In his speech, Douglass refuted this view and stressed the need for continued watchfulness and agitation.